INTRODUCTION

On one occasion I remembered to expound on Econet and, as I was perusing generally, I saw an example and it was the way Strive Masiyiwa brings in cash, and even how his organization, Econet, utilizes a similar technique to make money.

To realize how Strive Masiyiwa brings in cash or how he brought in cash, don't waste your time looking at Econet's various products or even the mobile telecommunications network itself and counting the millions or billions of dollars because all you will see is beauty that is skin deep; look at Econet as an entrepreneurial activity starting from the beginning and dissect it from there.

If you take a gander at Econet all along and as a pioneering action instead of a portable broadcast communications organization, you will see that Strive Masiyiwa and Econet's multibillion dollar recipe is certainly not a versatile media communications network at all.

While investigating and perusing many reports, the image of how Strive Masiyiwa made and brings in his cash started to come to fruition in my mind until I had the full picture and I was persuaded this was it.

I was extremely certain of it however I simply required some additional supporting proof. The proof would come as the Econet 2011 Annual Report.

Looking at one page of Econet's yearly report, it was so self-evident, and Econet's, and at last Strive Masiyiwa's multibillion dollar recipe was gazing at me squarely in the face. It was not clearly, but rather it was not too far off in the open and I could see it.

When I saw it I laughed.

Like I said in my first book, Turning Iron into Gold: Golden Opportunities: How to Spot Them, Create Them, Make Money from Them, and How Not to Miss Them, once in a while to observe an open door you need to peruse between the lines.

From that day onwards I let anybody know who minded to listen that, "Assuming you give me one base station I won't neglect to bring in cash. Everything I will do is placed it in Harare and I won't neglect to make money."

Harare is the capital city of Zimbabwe and the most populated city in Zimbabwe.

Sadly nobody simply gives you a base station for free.

That's the place where the contrast between Strive Masiyiwa and Econet Wireless, and the vast majority is. Masiyiwa had the option to get the gear and to begin the business.

You see, you can have a similar plan to bring in cash, or even duplicate it, yet there are different variables that become an integral factor that different the quality goods from the waste, or the harvest from the weeds, or the men from the young men, or the harsh from the riff-raff.

CHAPTER 1: GENESIS: IN THE BEGINNING

Before setting up Econet, Masiyiwa worked at the state-possessed Posts and Telecommunications Corporation (PTC) (of Zimbabwe) where he didn't oversee cell organizations. PTC was a proper line administrator, and it didn't have a cell (versatile) network. There had not been a cell network in Zimbabwe at that time.

Masiyiwa had no earlier innovative experience working for a versatile broadcast communications organization, and he had never set up a portable media communications company.

When I express "set up a portable media communications organization", I mean from ground up, I don't simply mean setting up steel towers which Zimbabweans themselves could accomplish for a really long time, yet I mean setting up a working portable media communications network with the center GSM advances, steel pinnacles and charging frameworks to boot.

There had not been a portable broadcast communications organization in Zimbabwe previously and Masiyiwa didn't have the experience, so how did Masiyiwa pull it off?

How did he kick Econet off and going?

To set up a portable media communications organization, Masiyiwa required individuals who had done it previously and could rehash it; the experts.

CHAPTER 2: SETTING UP THE CELLULAR NETWORK

If you take a gander at the historical backdrop of Econet, you will see that since the establishing of Econet, L.M. Ericsson of Sweden has provided Econet with technology.

L.M. Ericsson is a goliath Swedish media communications innovation organization usually alluded to just as Ericsson.

If you have the cash to pay Ericsson, Ericsson can plan and build a versatile broadcast communications network for you from ground up; base stations, towers, charging frameworks and all; that you should simply turn on the organization by basically squeezing a power button and individuals can begin settling on decisions on your portable organization. Truth be told, Ericsson can plan and build the organization to the level where the organization is running and afterward pass on it for you to make the first call.

Econet was not Ericsson's first customer.

By the time Ericsson (1) supplied its technology to Econet, and (2) got its engineers on the ground in Zimbabwe to help set up Econet's mobile telecommunications network, it had already gained a lot of experience designing, rolling out, and even upgrading large and world-class mobile networks across the world, including in the developed world.

Ericsson sells telecommunications technologies like switches, base stations, etc., but it also offers its clients services that help sell Ericsson equipment, services like doing upgrades, designing and constructing mobile telecommunications networks etc., services that help Ericsson sell its products and make more money.

Some of the things Ericsson says on its site are really fascinating.

Among the administrations Ericsson says it offers are:

- Managed Services
- Consulting and Transformation
- Learning Services
- Network Design and Optimization
- Network Roll-
- Out Support
- Systems Integration

On "Organization Design and Optimization" [1], Ericsson says, "We offer a full scope of administrations tending to everything from innovation sending, network change, and organization streamlining to guarantee an ideal client experience and administrator profitability."

Services under "Organization Design and Optimization" include:

- *Network Planning* - "Network Planning includes traffic forecasting and capacity planning to balance network investments and network performance."
- *Network Design* - "With our Network Design service, you set the parameters for your network architecture, so it fulfills your business plan in terms of capacity, coverage, cost and quality of service."
- *Network Tuning* - "Network Tuning includes services to initially adjust the network before commercial launch. When a new network is installed or new features activated, the radio network functionality and operation ... "

Oh indeed, as displayed in the primary rundown, Ericsson likewise offers "Organization Roll-Out" as a service.

The above are only a portion of the administrations Ericsson offers on top of providing media communications network gear.

As you can see, regardless of whether you are an instructor like Jack Ma, and not so much as an architect, you also can have a completely working versatile media communications network going in the event that you can raise the assets to pay Ericsson to plan and build the versatile broadcast communications network for you.

CHAPTER 3: A MOBILE NETWORK OPERATOR

Now, Econet is a portable broadcast communications network administrator, and in addition to a portable media communications organization. A versatile broadcast communications network administrator "works" a portable organization so to say. A versatile telecoms network administrator could conceivably claim the portable media communications network it uses.

For instance, Econet Wireless South Africa is a portable virtual organization administrator (MVNO) where Econet is a versatile organization administrator that utilizes Cell C's portable media communications organization. Econet Wireless South Africa is as yet a portable administrator, however it doesn't possess the versatile media communications network framework it utilizations to give versatile organization telephone administrations in South Africa.

In Zimbabwe, Econet's portable broadcast communications network is only one piece of the Econet business very much like Google's site is the mechanical piece of Google the business.

There is a colossal distinction between Econet the business and Econet's portable broadcast communications network infrastructure.

A mobile telecoms operator like Econet must have organizational systems that include customer services, sales, marketing, finance, human resources management, legal/lawyers, etc., that support the operation of the mobile telecommunications services business as a whole.

As you read what is coming straightaway, recall the thing I said about Ericsson in the last sections in light of the fact that the technique is unraveling.

Also recollect what I said in the presentation, that assuming you gave me a base station I wouldn't neglect to bring in cash, I would just put it right at the focal point of Harare and give network cover over the entire of Harare and quickly begin making money.

Once Econet Wireless and the core mobile telecommunications network was set up and operational, small as it was then, it was immediately possible for the public to make calls on the Econet network and for Econet to start making money selling airtime. Econet would proceed to send off different administrations based on top of the center organization and endorser base.

Masiyiwa didn't concoct versatile media communications, neither did he foster programming for it, yet he brought in cash in the portable media communications industry.

That is something vital to know.

As you read what follows, recall the thing I said about Ericsson for the technique is unraveling.

You will see a fascinating pattern.

CHAPTER 4: FINANCIAL SERVICES

LIFE INSURANCE: ECOLIFE

EcoLife was a brand result of Econet that offered free extra security front of up to US$10 000 to Econet's prepaid supporters who spent at least US$3 each month.[2] When the EcoLife supporter passed on, the protection cover was paid out to the supporter's closest relative or beneficiaries.

I said "EcoLife was a brand result of Econet" for a reason.

With EcoLife, Econet was selling an innovation based help under its own image name, EcoLife, in the very way that Econet sells paid ahead of time broadcast appointment under its Buddie brand.

Within 5 months of's first experience with general society, before the finish of February of 2012[3], EcoLife had 1.2 million clients, every one of them solely Econet subscribers.[4]

Those 1.2 million EcoLife clients were utilizing a reliable measure of cash on the Econet network consistently to get life cover.

Econet was doing thundering

business! So how did Econet pull

it off?

Well, the product, the innovation used to make and work EcoLife was authorized (leased) to Econet by a Namibian organization called Trustco Mobile (Pty) Ltd.[5] The product was a result of the Namibian organization. Econet paid Trustco Mobile permit charges (sovereignties) to utilize Trustco Mobile's product. Trustco Mobile's product made it workable for Econet to offer its supporters broadcast appointment use based disaster protection cover.

The agreement to utilize Trustco Mobile's product was endorsed among Econet and Trustco Mobile in August 2010 and EcoLife was sent off in October of that very year. The agreement would lapse in February 2012[6]. So it took Econet only three months to carry EcoLife to the market.

Trustco Mobile gave the "broadcast appointment utilization based protection" innovation to Econet and Econet proceeded to create huge amount of cash. Trustco's broadcast appointment utilization based programming was essentially associated with Econet's

business frameworks that track broadcast appointment use rejuvenating EcoLife on Econet's network.

The help given by Trustco Mobile's innovation received Econet's clients reliably burning through cash on broadcast appointment as a trade-off with the expectation of complimentary life insurance.

Econet even got new clients in view of EcoLife.

Just like toward the start with Ericsson, here we see Econet getting innovation from an innovation organization (Trustco), marking the assistance the innovation gives, and doing a rewarding business with that technology.

MOBILE MONEY: ECOCASH

In September of 2011, Econet sent off its versatile cash move administration called EcoCash.[7]

EcoCash permitted "EcoCash-enrolled" Econet clients to utilize their cell phones to send and get money.

EcoCash fills in as follows. You give an EcoCash specialist the cash you need to store into your versatile wallet, EcoCash, very much like keeping cash into your financial balance. The EcoCash agent will then enter the value of the money in your EcoCash account (mobile wallet), and from there you can send money from your mobile wallet (EcoCash account) to another cellphone number, or use it to pay for purchases wherever EcoCash is accepted.

Mobile cash isn't a media communications item however a monetary item that utilizes media communications innovation the same way a wire move, transmitted move, or an internet based installment utilizes media communications technology.

So how did Econet pull it off?

Econet had no portable cash insight, it was only a media communications organization and Masiyiwa was never a banker.

So how did Econet pull it off?

Well, before Econet was sent off EcoCash in Zimbabwe, Econet previously worked a versatile cash administration called EcoKash in Burundi. Notwithstanding, yet, Econet went into the versatile cash business in Burundi with no related knowledge of running such a service.

I will educate you concerning what Econet did in Zimbabwe since that is the place where Econet began its business yet operates.

EcoCash wasn't the main cash move administration in Zimbabwe. It was a newbie, and before it there was eTranzact's portable cash administration, NetOne's OneWallet, and Kingdom Bank's Cellcard.

EcoCash ran on top of Econet's framework and it utilized Econet's supporter base to turn into the biggest cash move administration in Zimbabwe.

So, how precisely was Econet ready to offer a versatile cash administration in Zimbabwe?

Well, by 2011, a South African innovation organization called Pattern Matched Technologies had fostered a versatile cash administration innovation that permits any portable organization administrator that needs to begin a portable cash administration to do as such. The portable cash administration innovation from Pattern Matched Technologies is called Amethyst and around then, by 2011, it was at that point being used in different nations. Amethyst permits clients of a portable organization to send and get versatile cash and even do things like their versatile wallet total etc.

Econet got Pattern Matched Technologies' Amethyst portable cash item, associated it to its organization, and sent off EcoCash, its portable cash administration, in September 2011.

Econet was presently in the portable cash business.

Just like in the first place where Ericsson was the innovation provider, Pattern Matched Technologies needed to do everything to ensure that its product worked faultlessly with the business frameworks of its client, Econet, and it brought to the table for designing help administrations or potentially carry out Amethyst for the client as a feature of the entire deal.

You see, items like portable organization stuff and portable cash programming are capital items; items that are utilized to create an item the business sells. Portable cash programming, for instance, isn't similar to straightforward buyer programming that you introduce all alone with next to no assistance.

Mobile organization administrators have their current activities in question when they interface different frameworks to their center organization, so innovation providers frequently give the innovation as well as the specialized abilities to introduce the product and they even train the client on the best way to fill different roles etc.

In a news discharge proclaiming Econet's send off of EcoCash, Pattern Matched Technologies said;

"Econet wanted to send off this huge new framework by the end of September 2011, expecting to change the manner in which Zimbabweans trade merchandise. …

"PMT engineers worked indefatigably to guarantee that development of the entire framework is finished and accomplished its expected date of 30 September 2011."[8]

One year after the fact, in August 2012, Econet changed the EcoCash innovation from Pattern Matched Technologies' Amethyst to Mobiquity, a portable cash administration innovation of an organization from India called Comviva.[9]

In January 2013, Econet reported that EcoCash had got 2 million clients since origin. Econet likewise reported spending more than $50 million such a long ways on the EcoCash administration. [10] [11]

Sixteen months from send off, US$100 million was traveling through EcoCash consistently, converting into an annualized US$1.2 billion per year.

In September of 2013, two years in the wake of sending off EcoCash and one year in the wake of exchanging portable cash administration innovations, Econet would agree that the accompanying in a statement:

"Econet Wireless is embraced a multi-million dollar extension of its versatile cash administration, EcoCash, because of its emotional and startling development since its send off in September 2011.

"The development will make the EcoCash framework multiple times greater than it is as of now, and furthermore make ready for the organization to send off extra services.

"Chiefs at the organization yield they have been gotten off guard the sensational development of EcoCash, and have needed to scramble to arrange and introduce a lot greater framework. Engineers from the organization's providers have been in Zimbabwe for a long time overhauling every one of the frameworks and they are supposed to have finished their work before the finish of September."[13]

As you can see with your own eyes, Econet was provided with the innovation as well as the architects who might redesign the system.

Econet didn't concoct these advancements, however it proceeded to make huge loads of cash and make Masiyiwa rich utilizing advances made by others.

BUNDLES: FACEBOOK BUNDLES AND WHATSAPP BUNDLES

Econet has two group items; Facebook packs and WhatsApp packs. These are extremely fascinating minimal expense items with regards to a market that is tremendously cost sensitive.

At the hour of composing this book, rather than paying Econet US$50 to visit any site of your decision up to a furthest reaches of 2.5GB of information use, you can simply purchase a US$3 month to month Facebook pack (Facebook association) with access Facebook just and that's it. A similar applies to WhatApp packs where you can likewise pay $3 for a drawn out WhatsApp association. Week after week heaps of each go for US$0.95.

These bundle products and their prices are very attractive to Econet customers who do not have to also incur extra costs of software updates that may be happening in the background on their smartphones or on their computers when they go on Facebook or WhatsApp using their smartphones or computers.

The packs have been an out of control business achievement. So how did Econet pull it off?

Well, Econet got the bundles technology from a Canadian company called Sandvine, then the bundles technology was connected to Econet's network infrastructure, and then Econet created the two Econet-brand products; Facebook Bundles, and WhatsApp Bundles.; and Econet was in business.

In a press explanation in May 2014, Sandvine, the Toronto Stock Exchange-recorded innovation organization that gave Econet the packs programming said:

"Perceiving the chance for administration designs that lined up with supporter ways of behaving and drifts, Econet Wireless created and sent off a limitless WhatsApp pack, utilizing Sandvine's Usage Management arrangement executed with Sandvine's neighborhood accomplice Three6Five Technologies. The WhatsApp groups incorporates differing plans - 30 pennies everyday, 95 pennies each week and $3 per month - to offer scaled down Internet plans estimated to address the issues of the market demographic."

Sandvine happened to say:

"Since February 2014, the Unlimited WhatsApp pack has encountered enormous reception by Econet supporters, WhatsApp currently represents over 23% of organization movement. Econet's Unlimited WhatsApp group permits endorsers of offer photographs, recordings, voice notes, areas, documents and connections on the famous constant interchanges application, as frequently as they need at a decent cost each month, week or even per day."[14]

As you can see, Econet didn't create the packs innovation. All things being equal, Econet got the groups innovation from Sandvine and proceeded to rake in some serious cash with Facebook packs and WhatsApp bundles.

While on account of Mobiquity, the versatile cash programming, it was the provider whose architects chipped away at the execution/overhaul; on account of groups it was Sandvine's neighborhood accomplice that carried out the innovation to work with Econet's organization and Econet's business systems.

CHAPTER 5: THE BIG FINISH

Now, let us rewind.

Remember how I clarified that Ericsson gave the innovation and designers to set up Econet's portable network?

Now, notice how the innovation for EcoLife, the protection item, was obtained from a Namibian organization, Trustco, and how the Namibian organization gave the specialized ability. Very much like at the outset with Ericsson.

Next up is EcoCash.

Notice how with the versatile cash item the product was obtained from an innovation provider who then, at that point, carried out it and even proceeded to update it.

Next up is Facebook packs and WhatsApp groups.

Notice how Econet used Sandvine's Usage Management technology that was implemented, well, this time around by a local partner of Sandvine's.

So what do we have?

Well, we see a pattern here, the "method".

I call it "The Ericsson Method" because it is the same method by which Econet was set up.

Well, that's what I saw.

"The Ericsson Method" is still alive and kicking!

When I saw the pattern in Econet's entrepreneurial pursuits, I woke up to the reality that here is someone making billions of dollars using one simple formula while some folks spend forever trying to work on breakthrough technologies, just for the prestige of being called a technology entrepreneur, without any roaring financial success.

The day I discovered "the method" being applied in virtually all of Econet's entrepreneurial ventures I just laughed by myself.

Econet would later release its 2011 annual report showing logos of its "partners" who of course included Ericsson, Pattern Matched Technologies, and others. I laughed seeing the logos. From that day onwards their game was up. It was no surprise to me in 2014 that I would learn that the bundling technology for Facebook bundles and WhatsApp bundles was NOT created in-house by Econet. I only laughed some more!

The lesson I got from it all was simple; just make money!

Why bother creating new technologies when you can make billions of dollars right now using technologies you can source from specialists?

Not everyone can get filthy rich through developing innovative and breakthrough technologies. Some folks will get filthy rich using the technologies of others.

In my view, it is better to make the money, and then when you have billions of dollars at your disposal, start developing your own products in-house. After all, most start-ups with cutting edge technologies fail to get off the ground because of a lack of capital. Once you have accumulated sufficient capital and you can afford it, you can then develop revolutionary technologies. At that stage, you will be able to absorb some of the research and development costs without a dent on the viability of your business.

Take EcoLife and Trustco's software.

It took three months from the signing of the contract for EcoLife to be launched. If it took three months just to launch EcoLife, what more creating the software?

If you then add the time to develop and test the mobile money software, you will see that it will cost a lot of money, take a lot of time, and take skills that will take Econet away from its core areas of specialization. By getting the mobile money software from Pattern Matched Technologies, Econet was able to quickly enter the mobile money services market, and with a tried-and- tested mobile money solution.

In Zimbabwe the mobile money market was growing fast and Econet had to enter the mobile money market before it cost more to enter the market after a competitor has established dominance and strong brand loyalty. The fastest way for Econet to enter the market was to source the technologies from specialist providers of tried-and-tested mobile money technologies, instead of developing the technology inhouse.

CHAPTER 6: DEVELOPING OWN TECHNOLOGIES

Today, several years later, Econet invents things. Econet would not be able to do that today if it had not built its business to what it is today, and the way it did.

In a Monday 7 January 2013 news release, Econet would say:

"As with everything Econet does, the company commissioned detailed studies to try and ascertain how much it was losing in potential revenue, because its customers could not charge phones. The studies showed that it could generate an additional 25-30% in revenue by addressing the problem of charging for its customers.

"Econet not only found a solution for the problem, it did so by addressing an even bigger problem for ordinary people when there is a power cut; providing simple lighting. So Econet put a team together to develop a solar powered lantern that could also charge a cell phone.

"The company first tried various off-the-shelf products from China but found them unreliable. So it set up its own business in China and began not only to supply lanterns to its own businesses in various African countries like Zimbabwe, but also to other countries where it does not even operate."[15]

So there you have it, from "off-the-shelf products" to internal product research and development, and of course studies showing just how much extra revenues would be generated.

CHAPTER 7: ONE MORE THING

I wrote the first unedited draft of the preceding chapters sometime mid-2014, before the Sandvine announcement, and by then I had made the cover which I posted on my Facebook page. There is a very important announcement that both Econet and Ericsson made in November 2014 that fit perfectly into this book. The announcement was about the signing of a 5 year deal between Ericsson and Econet.

In the announcement on Monday 24 November 2014, Ericsson said:

"Ericsson (NASDAQ:ERIC) today announced that it has been selected as the sole supplier by Zimbabwe's largest provider of telecommunications services, Econet Wireless Zimbabwe, for the company's Core network upgrade program. The deal will see the companies working together to simplify and upgrade the existing 2G/3G/4G/LTE networks, future proofing it for the rapid mobile expansion in the country.

"Bernard Fernandes, Group CTO of Econet says: "We have chosen our trusted long-term partner Ericsson to accompany us on this journey and look forward to the ability to launch new products and quality services to our customers."

"Building on the companies existing long-term partnership, the new scope will rationalize and upgrade the Core network as well as introduce the latest Ericsson network architecture.

"… In the Harare area, which currently carries more than half of all traffic on the network, the project will also upgrade the radio access network (RAN) to include Ericsson's multi-standard RBS 6000 family of base stations for macro and small cell networks.

"Pieter Goosen, Country Manager for Ericsson Zimbabwe, says: "Econet is the market leader in Zimbabwe and this project will give them one of the most advanced Core networks on the continent, providing them far more capacity to manage and scale their network."[16]

I had a jolly good
laugh. Their game was
up. "The Ericsson
Method."

LESSONS IN BUILDING A HIGHLY SCALABLE STARTUP AND A LARGE SCALE ENTERPRISE

I will now share some more lessons in building a scalable startup and a large scale enterprise in the coming chapters.

CHAPTER 8: ORGANIZATION-BUILDING SKILLS

Strive Masiyiwa could set up Econet Wireless, the business, because he had other skills or competencies which not everybody has, but certainly others do, skills to put all the parts together and have a mobile telecommunications network running; organization-building skills, skills to organize parts of the whole so that they build one larger unit and function as one larger single unit.

When I say "parts" I mean things like raise startup capital, assemble the team, and even get lawyers to fight for the mobile telecommunications licence etc. until Econet could function on its own even without Masiyiwa.

At this stage I am talking of setting up and building Econet, organizing the business.

A functional mobile telecommunications network infrastructure is just one part of the business.

A licence to operate a mobile telecommunications network is also one part of a business.

Owning a working mobile telecommunications network infrastructure is just one aspect of the business.

A business is much more than just the things it owns; it is a combination of internal component systems.

If, for example, you remove Econet's entire customer service staff today and you don't replace them, it would not be long before the company goes down.

An organization or business like Econet is a combination of organizational systems, a combination of parts of the whole working together as a combined system.

It takes organization-building skills to build and combine all those component systems into a larger self-sustaining system.

CHAPTER 9: A BUSINESS

Every business is a combination of systems that make it in the same way a human body is a combination of systems that include the nervous system, the blood circulation system, the endocrine system, the digestive system, skeletal structure, etc.

Although there are other entrepreneurs besides Strive Masiyiwa who have started mobile telecoms companies, not many people possess such skills to get all the parts together, and put them together so that those parts work as one business unit; a single functional business entity.

Some folks can raise all the funding a mobile network operator can ever need, but they cannot combine different parts to build their own mobile telecommunications business. Some engineers are experts at engineering, and that's where their skills end; they cannot start a specialist engineering business of their own because they do not have the skills to put all the parts together and get them working as one functional and sustainable business entity. That is why not everybody can start a business like Econet, at least the way Masiyiwa did it. It's all about organization-building skills.

CHAPTER 10: DEVELOPING ORGANIZATION-BUILDING

SKILLS

Before starting Econet, Masiyiwa started and ran a successful engineering/construction business called **Retrofit**. So Masiyiwa had practical organization-building skills and experience, although from the construction/engineering sector. Retrofit would handle large-scale engineering contracts. This provided a base for Masiyiwa to learn and even gain experience in starting and scaling a company as well as manage large-scale projects.

Also relevant is the fact that Masiyiwa had prior work experience working for a large telecommunications business, the state-owned Posts and Telecommunications Corporation.

These experiences, light as they may seem, helped develop his organization-building skills.

CHAPTER 11: TEACHING AN ORGANIZATION ENTREPRENEURSHIP

Masiyiwa was able to gather and assemble all the components together and get Econet going from almost nothing, which is what entrepreneurs do.

As Masiyiwa got Econet off the ground, he, in the process, taught Econet an entrepreneurial approach that Econet would copy and later apply to generate lots of money, even today.

So how did that happen? When did he do that? How did he create a culture?

Well, when Masiyiwa was setting up Econet, he built a team, team-member by team-member, as he went along. When he was setting up the network infrastructure, base stations and all, his team was involved; it was not a one-man show. As all this was going on and Econet was going through its development stages, Masiyiwa by consequence, created what would be Econet's entrepreneurial approach, an entrepreneurial blueprint, a method, an entrepreneurial stencil that Econet would use in the future. Masiyiwa's startup team saw how he was doing it and how everything was getting in place. The members of Strive Masiyiwa's original startup team would go on to occupy high-level executive posts in Econet as Econet grew, spreading Masiyiwa's entrepreneurial approach through the whole company even as it grew. As a result, Masiyiwa's entrepreneurial approach established itself as Econet's de facto approach to entrepreneurship and part of its corporate culture.

Even today those who join Econet will learn Econet's entrepreneurial approach when they participate in Econet's business development and roll out of new products and business units.

CHAPTER 12: GROWING THE BUSINESS

Econet started small with no subscribers and ended its first year of business with 32 000 subscribers.[17]

So, how is it then, that Econet now has over 9 million subscribers?

From a technical point of view, larger numbers of subscribers have only been able to be accommodated through network upgrades and expansion. From a marketing point of view, larger subscriber numbers have been achieved through heavy marketing. From a financial point of view, Econet has been able to grow to 9 million subscribers through its ability to raise funds for operations and network expansion. From a sales point of view, Econet got 9 million subscribers by selling 9 million sim cards. Take Ecocash, within 2 years, Econet spent over US$50 million on EcoCash alone. On the ground Econet established the largest mobile money agent in the country. Brand visibility of EcoCash was very high. While it may look like it was only the marketing department that did all the work, engineers and sales people and lawyers and many others were part of the success, it was a collective effort.

So to understand how Econet got to have 9 million subscribers, one has to look at Econet as a co-ordinated collection of systems working to achieve 9 million subscribers, instead of looking at Econet's 9 million subscribers as having come from the effort of just one system.

When one looks at Econet, scaling up (growing) the network capacity of the technology-based company has always involved upgrades. These upgrades have been done with the assistance of technology suppliers like Ericsson and others. As we have seen before, even add-on services like mobile money have been introduced, grown, and upgraded with the assistance of an outside technology supplier. Companies like Ericsson do offer training for their products. So in the process there has been skills transfers from the technology companies to Econet to the extent that when a problem arises on the Econet network, Econet can simply call its own engineers rather than call Ericsson. These Econet engineers, are part of the system and they work with other systems or functional areas within Econet to

achieve Econet's goals.

From an entrepreneurial point of view, one can see that Strive Masiyiwa's entrepreneurship model and Econet's entrepreneurship model is very simple and combines a few elements together. However, just because it looks simple it doesn't mean it is easy to do in practice.

As Econet has come to dominate the Zimbabwean mobile telecoms market with over 9 million subscribers, it is now focusing on increasing average revenue per subscriber through, for example, mobile money, WhatsApp bundles, and EcoLife.

CHAPTER 13: APPLICATIONS

What I have just shared can be a template for anyone to start a viable technology-based company and scale it. Most people who are not entrepreneurs but want to be entrepreneurs fail to become entrepreneurs because they see the end result of a technology-based company as well as its technological sophistication and even the capital-intensive nature of the business and begin to think they can't do it or even compete, when actually it's not that sophisticated and they can do it too so long as they are prepared to work hard. You do not have to manufacture base stations and towers in order to start a mobile network operator. Neither do you have to be an engineer.

CHAPTER 14: CROSS-POLLINATION

Before starting Econet, Masiyiwa was in the construction industry through his company called Retrofit.

In the construction industry there is something called a turnkey project. What happens in a turnkey construction project is that a construction company will build a whole building to completion with water, electricity, air conditioning, and painting all included that at the end of the project, the customer will just get keys to immediately start using the building.

The turnkey project-management model can be crossed over to the mobile telecommunications industry and other large scale projects of a utility nature such as power, petrochemicals, and water for example.

Even if you are not an engineer or a scientist, there are entrepreneurial approaches through which you can build a massive technology-based company. You do not necessarily have to do it yourself, or do everything yourself, or know everything.

CHAPTER 15: FOCUS

You must know what business you want to be in and what your business is, and how you are going to make money.

Econet's main business is selling airtime. Although Econet's business model is evolving with changes in the market and business realities, it started business selling airtime, which it still sells today.

You must be careful what you decide to be the business of your business from the outset because what you decide to be the business of your business will have a bearing on the cost of running that business and growing it, as well as its profitability.

Ericsson, for example, is in the mobile telecommunications business as a technology supplier and it makes money doing that. On the other hand, Econet uses the technologies of Ericsson to make and sell airtime and Econet is very successful doing that. There are also other businesses in the mobile telecommunications industry like Comviva, Pattern Matched Technologies, and Trustco that make money just making software for the mobile network operators like Econet.

If your business is to sell water to homes, you do not necessarily have to be in the business of constructing dams. You can get the dam constructed by a specialist dam construction company with the waterworks to boot. If your business is a train service, you do not necessarily have to build your own trains and track. Econet is a mobile network operator, and it does not necessarily have to make its own mobile money software to be successful.

For a business to be competitive, it does not have to do everything because those specialist companies that focus on just one thing will do that one thing better than the business that does hundreds of things.

When you start a business from scratch, it is best that it is just focused on one area of the industry. In the vast majority of cases, it is not wise for a business to start off diversified doing this and that everywhere. Even investors will shy away from a company that looks like it has no direction and is a jack of all trades and a master of none. For years Econet focused on selling airtime and growing its market share; the subscriber base, sales, and network coverage. Once Econet dominated the market and network coverage covered virtually all of Zimbabwe, it began to branch into other areas,

building businesses and services like mobile money and mobile internet on top of its already existing subscriber base and infrastructure. Doing one thing at a time also works. The stage of development of your business should just tell you what to do and what not.

CHAPTER 16: METHOD

You must have a method for scaling (growing) your startup into a large-scale enterprise. In this text I have talked about how Masiyiwa and Econet did it. Every billionaire has a method of making money and every startup has a method of scaling. Find what works for you and your startup business.

Many entrepreneurs wonder how they can grow a small business into a large business.

Strive Masiyiwa and Econet essentially use the same entrepreneurial method throughout, even to get skills and capital.

I call it "the Ericsson method" because of Ericsson's involvement in building the core of Econet's network.

It is simply a modular-style of entrepreneurship where you get a core and connect other components to it to build something bigger. In fact, the core itself would be outsourced.

In the case of Econet as a whole, the core module is the mobile network infrastructure.

EcoCash, EcoLife, etc., are simply components that are added to the core. While this is more evident at the product and services level, it is also true at organizational (functions) level.

Econet has recruited people with specialist skills, and by specialist skills I mean specialist skills.

Want to raise US$100 million like Econet?

Then hire the people who have experience raising US$100 million. There is a difference, for example, between a qualified financial director, and a qualified financial director who can raise US$100 million all at once. Skills I said, and not just education!

I will just momentarily discuss the abilities of a portion of Econet's at various times directors.

Among a portion of Econet's over a wide span of time chiefs are; Tawanda Nyambirai, Nigel Chanakira, and Dr James Patrick Myers.

Nigel Chanakira began a bank, Kingdom Bank. Concerning Tawanda

Nyambirai and Dr James Patrick Myers, I will simply statement an Econet official statement gave at the hour of Dr Myers joining the Econet board:

"Dr Myers is a resigned previous Vice President for Africa of South Western Bell, presently part of AT&T, the world's biggest telecoms organization by esteem. he likewise filled in as the President of South Western Bell International Development Africa (Pty) Ltd from 1985 to 1998 and furthermore filled in as its Eecutive Vice President from 1994 to 1995. …

"He is additionally an advisor and has more than 30 years of worldwide business experience represent considerable authority in the media communications industry.

"Dr. Myers has a BA in Mathematics from Texas A&M University, a Master of Arts in Mathematical Physics from the University of Arizona and a Doctor of Philosophy in Industrial Engineering/Operations Research from Texas Tech University. He originally came to noticeable quality in Africa when he drove the group that obtained MTN South Africa in the mid 1990s for the monster American organization before it later sold it. From that point onward, he drove a consortium, which included Malaysia Telecom, that controlled Telkom South Africa for some years.

"In a concise explanation, on the takeoff of Mr Nyambirai from the board, Econet Wireless originator, Mr Strive Masiyiwa, said: "Tawanda Nyambirai has made an uncommon showing for us. He drove the lawful group that battled for the first permit in the courts. He has regulated the advancement of the business since the time I left Zimbabwe 12 years ago.""[18]

See, above Econet says it recruited Dr Myers who [emphasis mine], "drove the group that procured MTN South Africa in the mid 1990s for the monster American organization before it later sold it. From that point forward, he drove a consortium, which included Malaysia Telecom, that controlled Telkom South Africa for some years."

One of Econet's techniques for supporting its worldwide development is consortiums. Econet doesn't have all the cash on the planet. Econet's consortiums have up to this point been organizations organized so that Econet has a shareholding and the administration agreement to deal with the versatile telecoms business under the Econet brand and brand names, while different investors give the assets and let Econet manage everything. Econet utilized this technique when it entered Nigeria.

Setting up consortiums is an expertise all alone and when you have encountered individuals who have done it before in your camp, your organization can raise assets through framing consortiums on the grounds that your colleagues would

have done it previously. The greater the financing a colleague has raised through a consortium(s) previously, and the more consortiums he/she has driven, the better a resource he/she is to an organization that needs huge monies to support its startup as well as expansion.

There are numerous Texas A&M University BA in Mathematics graduates, yet the number of them have abilities have driven significant acquisitions and driven consortiums?

So, assuming you are a business person and you will require large cash, telecoms mastery, and legitimate aptitude, make certain to accept gifted brokers, telecoms leaders, and legal counselors who have done enormous things previously. This is a similar measured style of business I have discussed albeit presently it is at a tasks level.

An association without anyone else is a framework very much like a versatile organization, so when you really want a part, you can simply add it in, and on the off chance that it is done performing or it isn't acceptable, you can eliminate it. The nature of the component(s) you add to the hierarchical framework will have a heading on a piece of, or the entire framework and the outcomes you will get.

Capital-serious organizations like versatile organizations call for heaps of cash, millions to billions of dollars and in the event that you enlist a 20-year-veteran whose profession best was raising US$15 000, when you want to raise US$100 million, you won't go exceptionally far and quick. The versatile telecoms business is likewise abilities concentrated instead of work escalated. Thusly, you need to get profoundly gifted parts to add to the core.

On a side note, there are a few financial backers that work in giving both capital and the talented groups to unpracticed business people with good thoughts so the business visionary's thought turns into a billion dollar organization. The financial backers I am discussing are investors. Next time you hear that a 18-year-old began and presently runs a multibillion dollar organization that has gotten investment financing, odds are extremely high that that unpracticed 18-year-old got subsidizing and a group of experienced administrators from the funding organization, and that group continued to assemble the 18-year-old's thought into a strong billion dollar organization. This happens a great deal in America, most broadly in Silicon Valley. The funding organization brings in cash from the development in the worth of its portions. Obviously, that is another method.

CHAPTER 17: HOW DOES ONE GET THE SKILLS TO ASSEMBLE ALL THE PARTS TOGETHER?

Believe me, they can't show you this at school. You need to learn and consummate the workmanship without help from anyone else through training. There are certain individuals for whom simply employing someone else is absolutely impossible or their brains. They intentionally and subliminally need to try not to employ somebody and would prefer to learn everything themselves so they can do everything themselves (to reduce expenses). An organization like Econet is too enormous for one man to do everything. Incredibly couple of individuals at any point got very rich working alone.

Even Oprah has staff.

Once you realize that you can't make it exceptionally huge alone, you need to begin learning the craft of building an association utilizing the best parts accessible, not the least expensive parts accessible. Assuming that you start with the very least expensive parts, you will soon enough realize which type of parts are awesome to get the best results.

As I have shared previously, Masiyiwa had an organization called Retrofit preceding beginning Econet. Simply the demonstration of beginning Retrofit and running it effectively honed Masiyiwa's association building skills.

But where did he get them? Where did he get the association building skills?

That we might discuss, however I have presumably that Retrofit arranged Masiyiwa for Econet.

All I will say is, you can master association building abilities and tweak them as you go, through training, really doing. You gain tons of useful knowledge by doing.

That's the reason apprenticeships are fruitful world over. Indeed, even John D. Rockefeller of Standard Oil and Sir Ernest Oppenheimer, the organizer of Anglo American Corporation, went through an apprenticeship-style learning process.

Through experience(s) of beginning a business without any preparation and running it,

whether to progress or disappointment, you will master association building abilities and things like what to do and what not to do, what works and what doesn't, and which approach works and which approach doesn't. It is frequently through such experience(s) that you foster your own equation for success.

Interestingly Masiyiwa's way reflects that of one time world's most extravagant man, John D. Rockefeller. Rockefeller began as a student at an item exchanging business. Later he turned into an accomplice in that business. Then he entered another industry, the sprouting and quickly developing oil industry. All that time, Rockefeller worked with directors, investors, and business people that when he began Standard Oil he had obtained and adequately created association building abilities through training and experience.

Masiyiwa worked for Posts and Telecommunications Corporation, then he went into business, then he wandered into another industry, the sprouting and quickly developing versatile broadcast communications industry.

Organization-building abilities include assembling the best parts. I accept one can get and adjust association building abilities through practice.

Take a PC. It's one thing to peruse how to gather a PC and one more to collect it in fact. Regardless of whether the book has pictures and everything, you can turn into a gifted PC constructing agent by really making it happen. Presently, your cerebrum will work the same way with regards to gaining and fostering your association building abilities. Through practice you will learn how to put all the components together and build an organization, and even better organizations. Therefore there are sequential business visionaries, individuals who start many organizations, and at times selling every one of them for millions or billions of dollars.

MaSiyiwa began a few associations, Retrofit, Econet Wireless Zimbabwe, Mascom Wireless, T.S. Masiyiwa Holdings, etc.

In Zimbabwe, Econet itself has opened branches and specialty units for EcoCash, EcoSure, Econet Broadband, EcoFarmer, etc..

Econet has even begun independent organizations to serve EcoCash and EcoSure. That multitude of innovative endeavors reduce to association building abilities and having created as well as gained association building abilities. You can acquire association building abilities through training. That is the reason some school dropouts are ridiculously wealthy today on account of organizations they began; many learn at work, and even from business inability to business disappointment, constructing endlessly better associations, until they become pros at building strong organizations.

Once you have calibrated your association building abilities in a specific type of big business, you can begin and maintain various organizations that are appropriate for the sort of association building abilities you have created or possess.

That's the reason most innovation/web business people can without much of a stretch beginning another innovation/web business rather than a mining organization. A mining business visionary won't struggle with setting up another mining endeavor. Likewise exactly the same thing with CEOs move solely inside weighty industry, banking, mining, fabricating, or the quick buyer merchandise (FMCG) industry. Their abilities will be profoundly produced for that size of association and that type of big business and entrepreneurship.

CHAPTER 18: A STARTUP RAISING MILLIONS OF DOLLARS

First of all, Econet was not the principal organization in Zimbabwe to raise a huge number of US dollars.

As an obvious truth, Econet raised huge number of dollars in Zimbabwe. There isn't anything incomprehensible about raising large number of dollars.

It is totally critical that you read and comprehend the following passage, short as it might be.

Econet, basically, works apparatus, gear, and charges its endorsers expenses to get to the administrations the hardware gives to its supporters. Purchasing versatile organization hardware is the same as purchasing a bus!

That said, Ericsson has provided Econet with gear since inception.

Now, when Econet was begun in 1998, organizations like Ericsson, Nokia, and Siemens were battling for worldwide portion of the overall industry and for their organization stuff to be the future norm. The thought the telecoms gear producers had was that once they supply a portable organization administrator with hardware, that versatile organization administrator will turn into their client for a long time, even many years, ensuring pay for the telecoms gear creator for a long time to come.

The portable organization administrator will return to get greater hardware to extend the organization, update the organization, etc. It's an old thought currently called "client lifetime esteem" where the worth of the client to a business is taken a gander at as going past the first or only one exchange. So as may be obvious, rivalry for business that will last the existence of a portable administrator like Econet was wild. The architects of the portable organization administrators would likewise be prepared in utilizing the stuff of the provider and become specialists at it that it would be hard for a versatile organization administrator to simply change gear providers. Whenever Ericsson provided Econet with gear in 1998, Econet turned into Ericsson's client for a long time to come, more than a decade.

Ericsson would be engaged with redesigning and extending Econet's

organization. Perceiving the client lifetime worth of a portable organization operator,

and out of the longing to overwhelm the stuff market, one of the manners in which the versatile telecoms network gear producers contended was by offering merchant funding with extremely alluring credit terms.

Among the many wellsprings of money for a versatile organization, or even a transport organization, is seller financing.

In its monetary report for the year finished 28 February 2014, Econet said it got advance offices from among others, Ericsson Credit AB and ZTE who are major worldwide telecoms players. Econet's 2014 yearly report showed that in 2010, Econet got merchant funding to the tune of over US$135 million from ZTE. In 2012, Econet had a credit office of US$39.9 million from Ericsson Credit AB, the money arm of Ericsson. Econet additionally got a US$8 million credit structure PTA, an institutional loan specialist, to purchase hardware. The insurance for that advance was the gear Econet would purchase with the money.

Like in the days when Ericsson, Nokia, and Siemens were battling for piece of the pie utilizing liberal seller funding terms, today new and rising Chinese portable media communications network hardware creators like Huawei and ZTE are utilizing liberal credit terms to enter the worldwide versatile telecoms network hardware market. It gets better with ZTE and Huawei where the state-possessed Chinese banks finance the acquisition of imports of Chinese products, including versatile organization gear. Take China Development Bank for instance, which renegotiated Econet's ZTE merchant supporting office to the tune of US$135 million in May 2012.[19]

I have up to this point outlined how Masiyiwa and Econet's business style is measured and I have shown how it applies even at functional level.

You don't need to do everything yourself, including raising assets. If you want to raise millions of dollars to grow your company fast, and you don't have the skills to raise millions of dollars yourself or you don't even have time to do everything yourself, then get a component that can do it and is a "perfect fit" into your organization. Enlist the "wonderful fit" modules for explicit capacities in the association. It resembles getting the right piece of a jigsaw puzzle. On the off chance that the association can't raise reserves inside or doesn't have the abilities, it can likewise move toward a trader bank or venture bank(s) to raise the assets for example.

A comparable utilization of a secluded style of business we see Masiyiwa and Econet applying is the thing is classified "bootstrapping" a startup.

Bootstrapping a startup includes getting a startup going using funding and resources from any source, mostly unorthodox sources like friends, suppliers, pre-orders, crowdfunding, personal savings, etc., all in order to get the startup started. Bootstrapping is not about how neat, nice, and cool the sources of funding looks; it's about raising the capital and getting the business off the ground. You can bootstrap any amount. You do not have to get all the capital from one source. Already I have even told you that Econet has raised funds for expansion by forming consortiums. That's bootstrapping!

Indeed Econet's startup capital was bootstrapped as it was raised from pre-orders of SIM cards, bank advances, posting on the Zimbabwe Stock Exchange, obligations, selling Retrofit, etc.

One of the elements of a business person is to track down arrangements and to assemble associations that track down arrangements. A business can't go exceptionally far assuming that its only intention is simply to bring in cash. A business brings to the table for arrangements in the entirety of its aspects and as a business person, it is your business to track down answers for your business.

There is a justification for why Econet has client assistance staff on top of deals staff. Econet can sell a sim card today, yet regardless of how wonderful the innovation, there will generally be a client who comes saying he has a problem.

An irate client can come into the shop breathing fire saying he has come from a long way away and the sim card doesn't work and it's neglecting to settle on decisions, not understanding that there is no broadcast appointment in the sim card. It will be the occupation of Econet client support staff to track down an answer for the client's grievance and to stay away from a similar issue from here on out. On the off chance that the business doesn't offer arrangements, it will not hold clients. Assuming a business quits contribution arrangements, clients will leave. Arrangements. Track down arrangements. Make arrangements and they will remain your clients who will continue to spend more.

CHAPTER 19: HOW DO YOU GROW A BUSINESS LIKE ECONET?

Incremental natural development, geographic market extension, and acquisitions.

Above I discussed how various parts, utilitarian regions in the association, saw from the eyes of that part, develop the business all in all. The practical regions develop the business as a co-ordinated collaboration, a bigger consolidated framework. Deals can sell more items. Promoting can advertise the items and track down new business sectors. Business advancement can track down more business open doors. The specialized part can redesign and extend the organization foundation. Finance raises the assets. Every one of these parts assumes a part in developing the business and not simply developing deals, network limit, specialty units, or the item range. Every one of the practical regions are interlinked. The practical regions should have the option to help the development that is required as well as completely support the other utilitarian regions for economical development to be achieved.

You can't, for instance, vigorously advance another item with lacking subsidizing. In a similar way, you can't sell more sim cards when the organization limit is full. The organization limit must be there with the goal that clients can settle on decisions and the business can bring in cash from those sim cards. Every single utilitarian region and emotionally supportive networks should work pair. You can't have one region developing while the rest linger behind. Along these lines, developing the association will include developing the limit of each practical region and developing every region of the business. That way the entire association grows.

As for Econet turning into a global, it was unavoidable assuming Econet doesn't mess around with development since Zimbabwe on its own has a restricted pool of customers.

When a portable organization accomplishes public inclusion, the main geographic market extension that can happen is to go past lines. It's the idea of the business. Econet isn't WhatsApp or Facebook which can serve its administrations to the whole globe from one topographical location.

The idea of the business to the side, business real factors and interests can compel you to extend past boundaries even prior to accomplishing full public coverage.

Although a Zimbabwean organization, Econet began its activities in Botswana, some time before accomplishing public inclusion in Zimbabwe. The thing is, the point at which a chance to get a permit to work a portable organization in an outside country goes along, it is best to get the licence first because the licence is what you will need to do business in that country for the next several years while at the same time blocking competitors from entering that geographic market for just as long. The permit likewise makes it simple for you to raise capital from financial backers as it allows you to work the sort of business you have been authorized to do.

CHAPTER 20: START SMALL

You don't have to get going huge. You can get going with little organization limit and grow.

Econet began little, working simply in Harare and with not such countless base stations and hardware as it does today.

You see, one of the slip-ups many individuals make is to think each enormous organization today began immense, all things considered.

Even when you look at the products that Econet has rolled out to date, Econet started small. Take 4G. 4G has been rolled out city by city and not "wholesale" throughout the country at one go. This is a classic entrepreneurial act of starting small. The same thing happened with GPRS, 3G, and mobile broadband.

Econet even started small with EcoCash, that's why it had to upgrade its systems to be able to accommodate more customers.

A few years ago, when the Econet network in Zimbabwe was congested during the hyperinflation days when calls got cheap thanks to price-controls, Econet had to upgrade its systems to take on more calls at a time and to accommodate more lines.

Your startup does not have to be big from day one, or to have the biggest network with unlimited capacity from day one. In the case of a mobile network operator, it does not have to be perfect in the sense of covering every inch of the country from day one and with plenty of excess idle capacity to withstand all the national call traffic ten times over.

Start small, but small enough to do a profitable business offering a high-quality service. Your startup business may be small but a reputation for a high-quality service will follow your business into the future.

On that note, the pursuit to be perfect from day one is what keeps many wannabe entrepreneurs from actually becoming entrepreneurs. The truth is sometimes you just have to do with what works so long as it works. The pursuit to do everything and be everything from day one like in the perfect dream is what causes many a startup to go under. Dreams are nice, especially big dreams, but they need to be shaped by market realities and business realities. You do not always have to make your dream come true exactly as it was in your dream, sometimes just dreaming of riches is a better dream.

CHAPTER 21: START OR BUILD A CASH-RICH BUSINESS

In the first place, it is obvious how a mobile telecommunications network operator makes money. It simply sells airtime (bills for calls) and it will make money. Econet is predominantly a pre-paid business that sells pre- paid airtime. You pay first and then you make a call. You don't call first and then get a bill at the end of the month.

The pre-paid model helps manage cashflow by bringing in the money first, rather than wait for money at the end of the month while incurring expenses. The pre-paid model helps you avoid incurring costs of recovering monies owed for calls already made. You also do not even need to waste precious time checking whether someone earns enough a salary to afford making calls or not. The pre-paid sales of airtime also helps recover capital invested, at the least cost and relatively faster.

Lack of cashflow is one of the biggest killers of startup businesses, no matter how large their startup capital is.

With the pre-paid model however, which is now the standard for mobile network operators throughout Africa and for the majority of paid online services, the business get paid first before providing the service. This is even true for Amazon when you buy shoes and other such things Amazon sells.

For a business to have any chance of success and survival, it needs to make money and at least cover its expenses.

Econet used the pre-paid model from day one. Even today most of Econet's products are sold on a pre-paid basis, even over the counter.

The sooner a dollar gets into the business, the sooner it can be used in the business to make more money.

A dollar received today is worth more than a dollar received tomorrow.

Econet borrows huge sums of money running into hundreds of millions of dollars to grow its business. It pays interest on these loans. When Econet receives a dollar for a service sold, that dollar can be invested in interest earning instruments or reinvested in the business to make even more money.

In January 2015, Econet introduced EcoSure, a micro-insurance product.

On 2 March 2015 Econet said [emphasis mine];

""We have a situation where families do not have to deal with the shock of unplanned funeral costs after the loss of a loved one," [Econet Wireless CEO Douglas Mboweni] said. Mr Mboweni said although the packages available ranged from those with premiums of 50c per month for a pay-out of
$500 to $5 per month for a pay-out of $5 000, the most popular package is the $1 per month, which has a pay-out of $1 000. The Econet boss also revealed that in keeping with the Econet tradition of rolling out many innovations around a new service, plans are well advanced to launch other insurance products."[20]

It is a well-known fact that insurance companies are cash rich businesses. Not every customer of an insurance company will claim insurance, so some of the money will stay with the insurance company. At the end of the day, insurance companies are designed to be profitable through managing claims. As long as the insurance company's sales of insurance are higher than the sum of claims it pays out and its operating costs, the insurance company will make a profit.

Because most insurance, like EcoSure, is pre-paid on a regular basis, the insurance companies have reasonably assured revenues and cash inflows.

Econet's pre-paid micro-insurance product, EcoSure, will add more money to the money Econet has been generating through airtime sales and other already existing Econet products.

EcoSure is simply a service add-on to Econet's already existing business. Econet is going to use its already existing infrastructure to sell the product. It is not going to be the same as starting a new insurance company with its own standalone offices and distribution system from scratch.

EcoSure is being sold through Econet's already existing systems.

For a business to thrive, it must have a healthy cashflow. While Econet's cashflow is healthy so far and reasonably guaranteed from airtime sales, the insurance product boosts cashflows at the least extra cost to Econet.

To understand the value of insurance to Econet's operations, look at Zimbabwe's National Social Security Authority, NSSA, is an insurance company, although a pension fund, that has invested millions of dollars in other companies.

NSSA gets the millions of dollars it invests from workers who contribute to NSSA. That is how NSSA is able to fund the construction of shopping malls and other expensive buildings as well as invest in companies like Econet.

However, unlike in NSSA contributions, Econet's EcoSure is not a pension contribution, so Econet gets to keep a lot of money, and given millions of EcoSure customers paying anything from US$0.50 to US$5, that's millions of dollars a month. Even after payouts of life insurance claims, Econet will still remain with a lot of cash.

Econet, being a business that has to make a profit, would obviously not create EcoSure at a cost of millions if it did not make business sense.

An insurance business is like a bank, only that in the case of an insurance business, "depositors" do not get back their money unless there is an incident covered by the insurance. If there is no incident, the insurance company keeps the money.

The extra cost of running EcoSure on Econet's already existing infrastructure is small, and smaller than the money EcoSure stands to generate annually for Econet for years to come.

But there is another not so obvious benefit to Econet.

Apart from forming consortiums, one of the ways Econet raises funds is through borrowing large sums of money, like US$135 million.

Institutional lenders like banks are often interested in the cashflow of the business when they are deciding whether to lend to a borrower or not, and if they are going to lend the money, how much to lend, based, of course, on the cash-generating capacity of the business that wants a loan.

The millions of dollars that will be generated by EcoSure will help boost Econet's ability to raise bigger sums of money using its already existing infrastructure as well as give Econet a bigger cash-generating capacity, while at the same time reducing the need to borrow money all the time through an increased ability to raise money internally through EcoSure.

At the time of writing, Econet has almost 10 million customers and over

1 million EcoSure customers. So far we have been told that the most popular EcoSure package is the US$1 package and that Econet acquired over 1 million EcoSure customers within 2 months. So Econet was already making over US$1 million from EcoSure, within just 2 months. If all 10 million Econet customers become EcoSure customers paying just US$1 a month, EcoSure will earn US$120 million a year for Econet. Even if we deduct operating costs and expenses, Econet will still remain with tens of millions of dollars, US dollars.

And Econet has one heck of a way of trying to keep you alive and healthy by all means. Econet customers have lately been getting SMS messages about how to stay healthy! The messages about avoiding Ebola have been so many that virtually everyone one on the Econet network now knows what to do if he/she suspects infection. Then there was another one about raiding the fridge.

Yes people die but given then stability of Econet's subscriber base, EcoSure will generate a lot of cash for Econet.

That's EcoSure, alone.

In the case of EcoCash, in the year to February 2014, EcoCash had handled transactions worth over US$3.1 billion, earning Econet US$44 million in fees.[21]

Given the above figure, I will just conclude by saying if you want to start an organization that will grow to be like Econet, make sure it has billion dollar potential. If it doesn't have billion dollar potential, you can always grow it using the method Masiyiwa grew Econet from a small network in Harare. Yes, in its first year Econet had 32 000 pre-paid subscribers. Today it has over 9 million subscribers.

EcoCash on its own is making tens of millions of dollars for Econet for Econet already, and EcoSure was a million dollar business within two months.

Lesson, start a business that becomes a million dollar business within two months.

May you prosper.